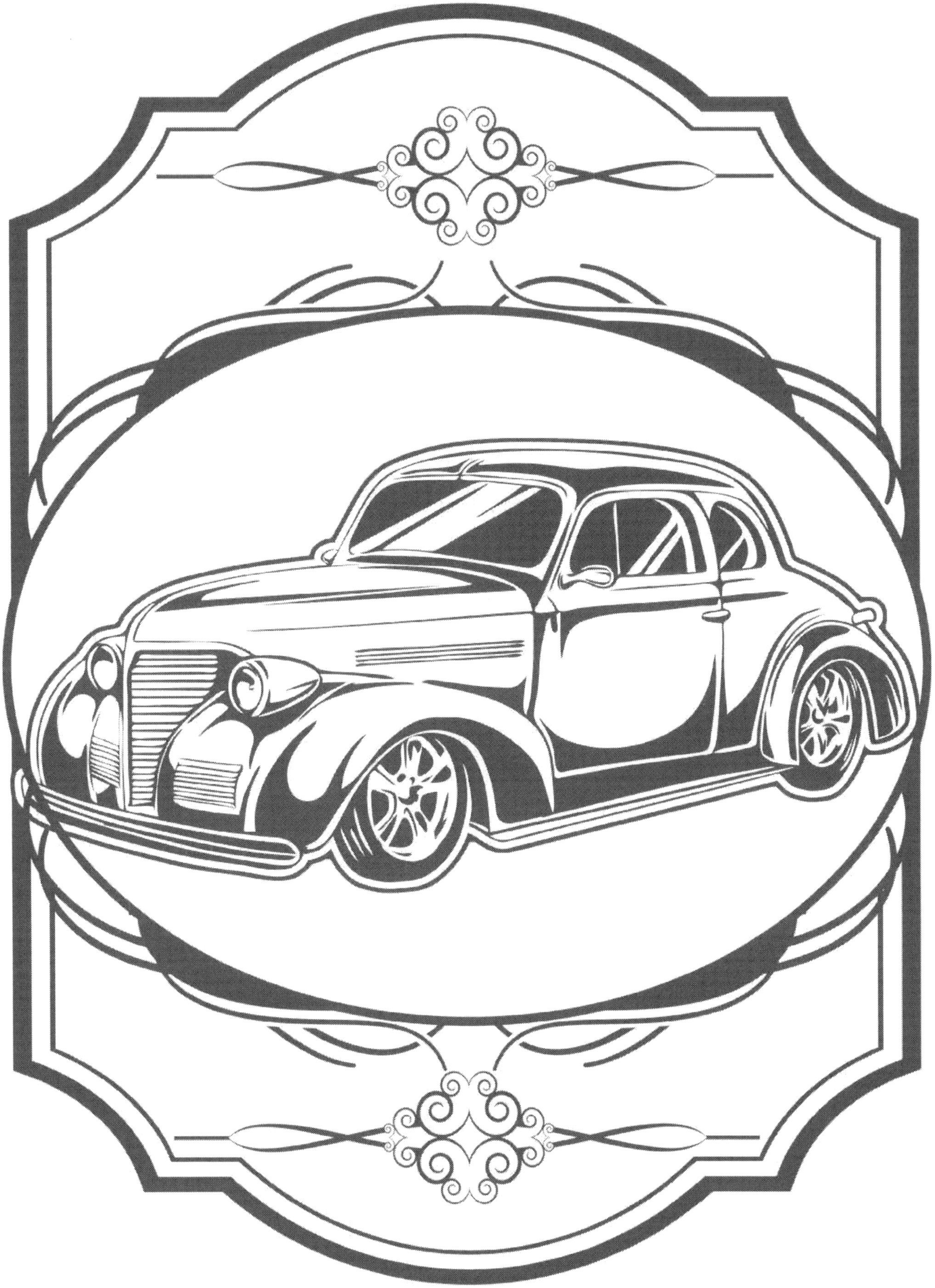

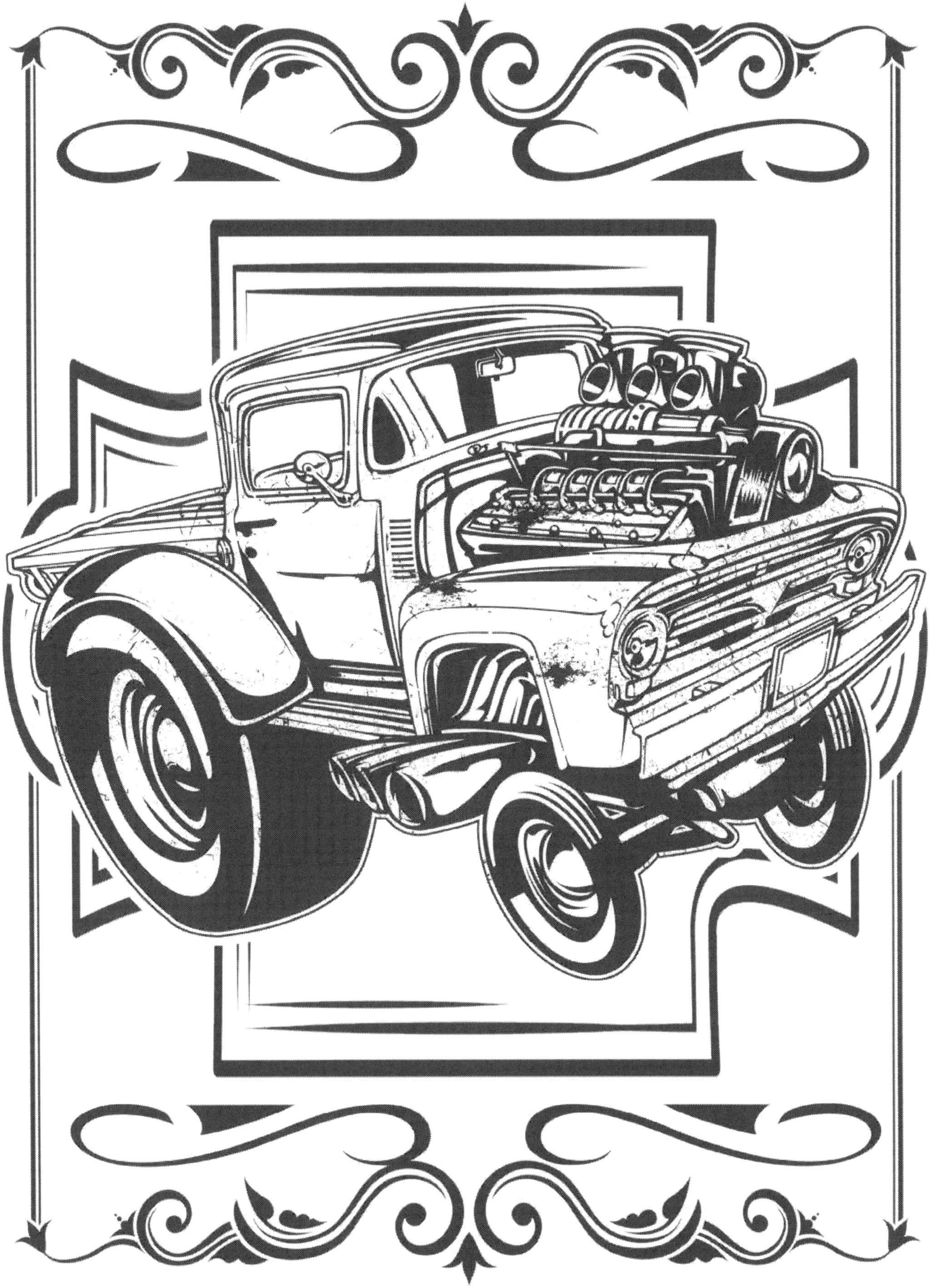

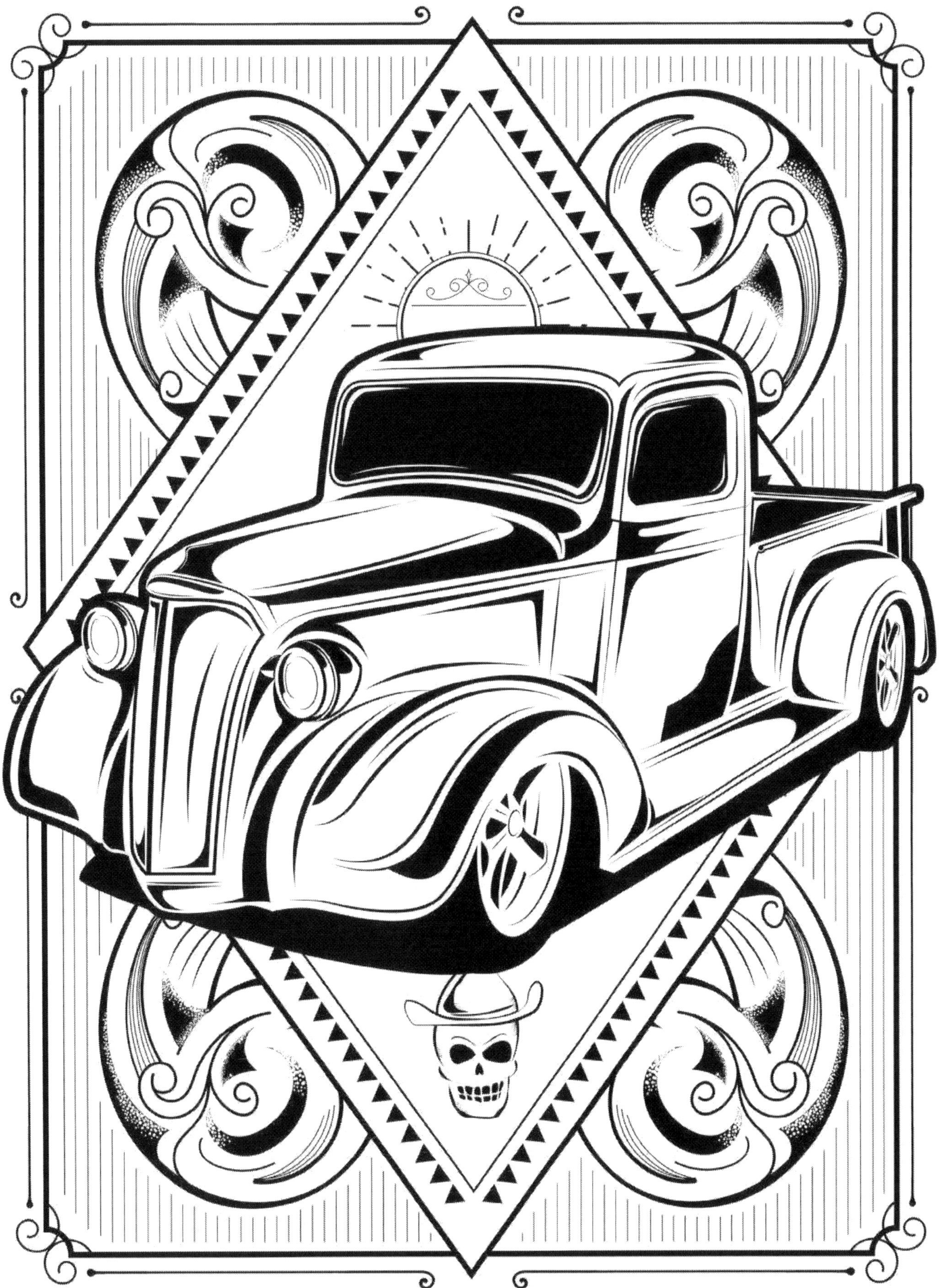

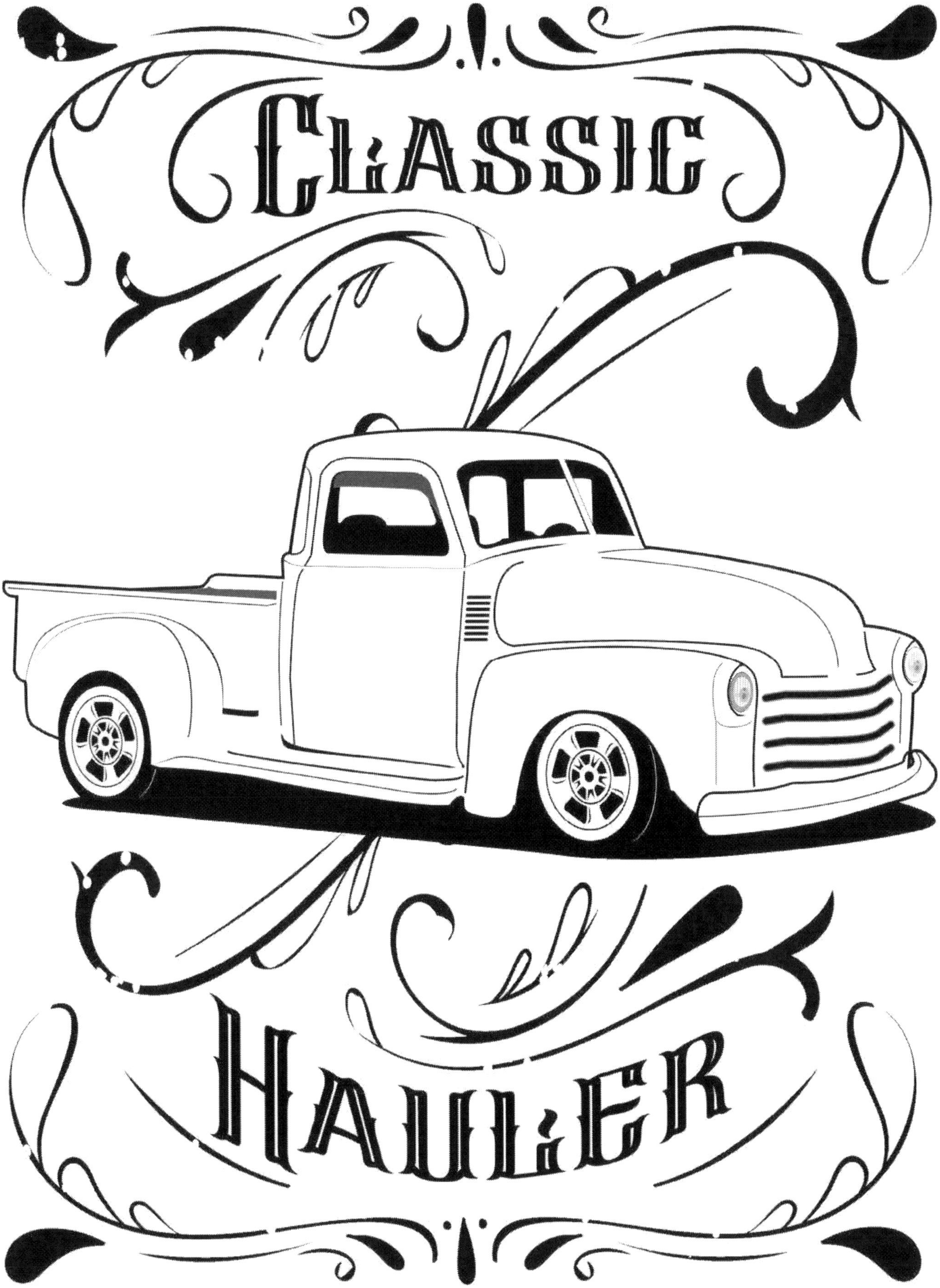
CLASSIC
HAULER

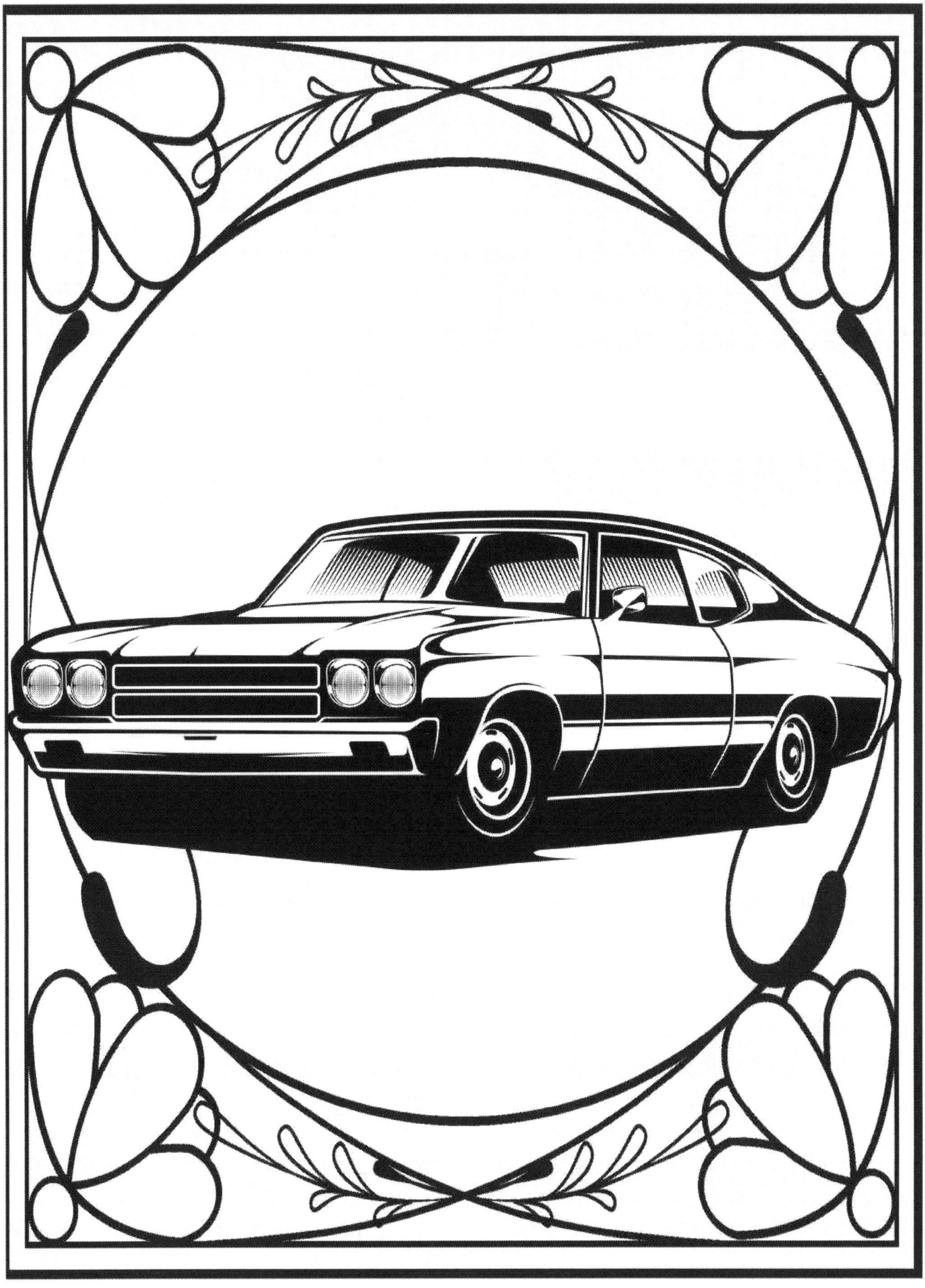

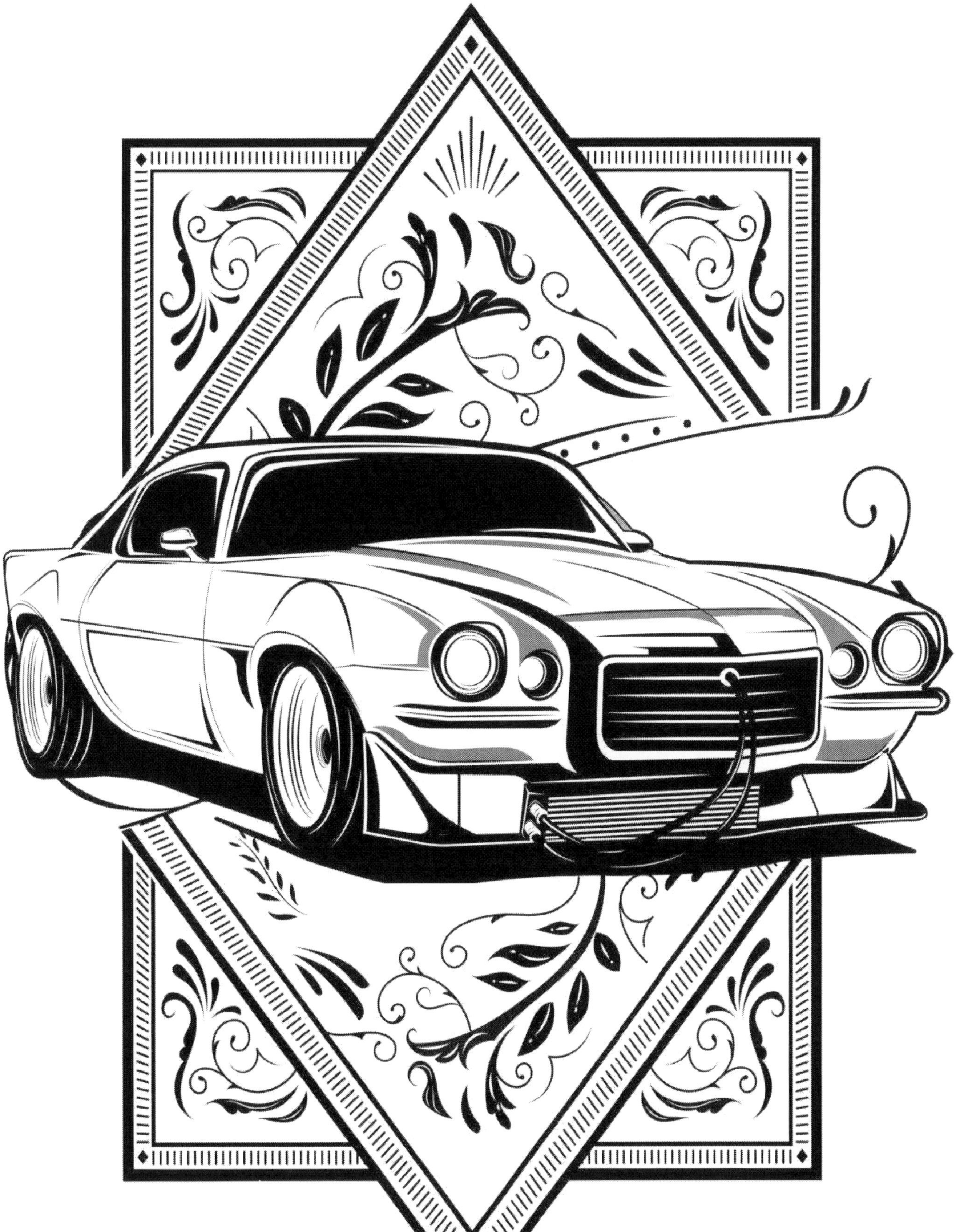

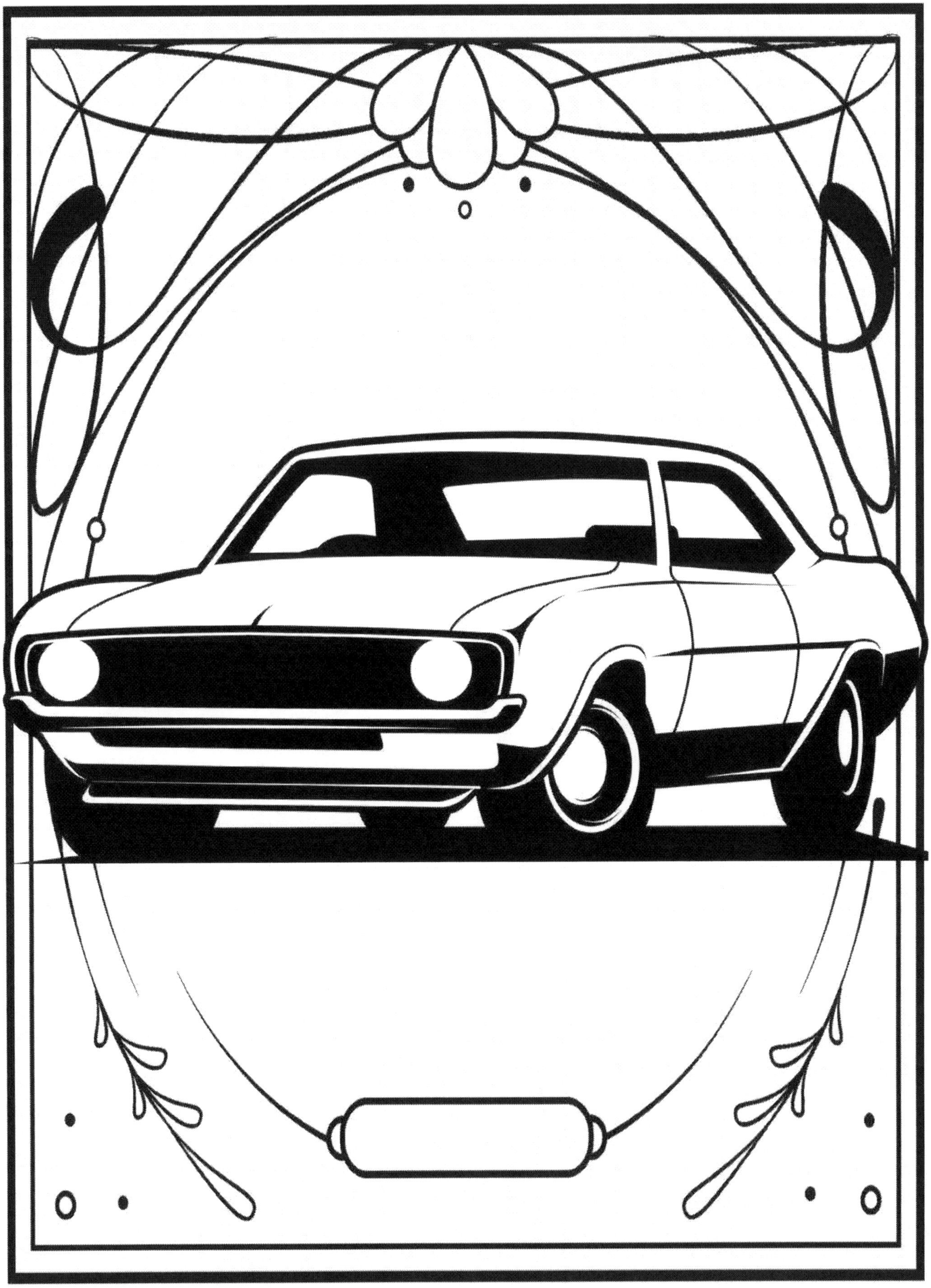

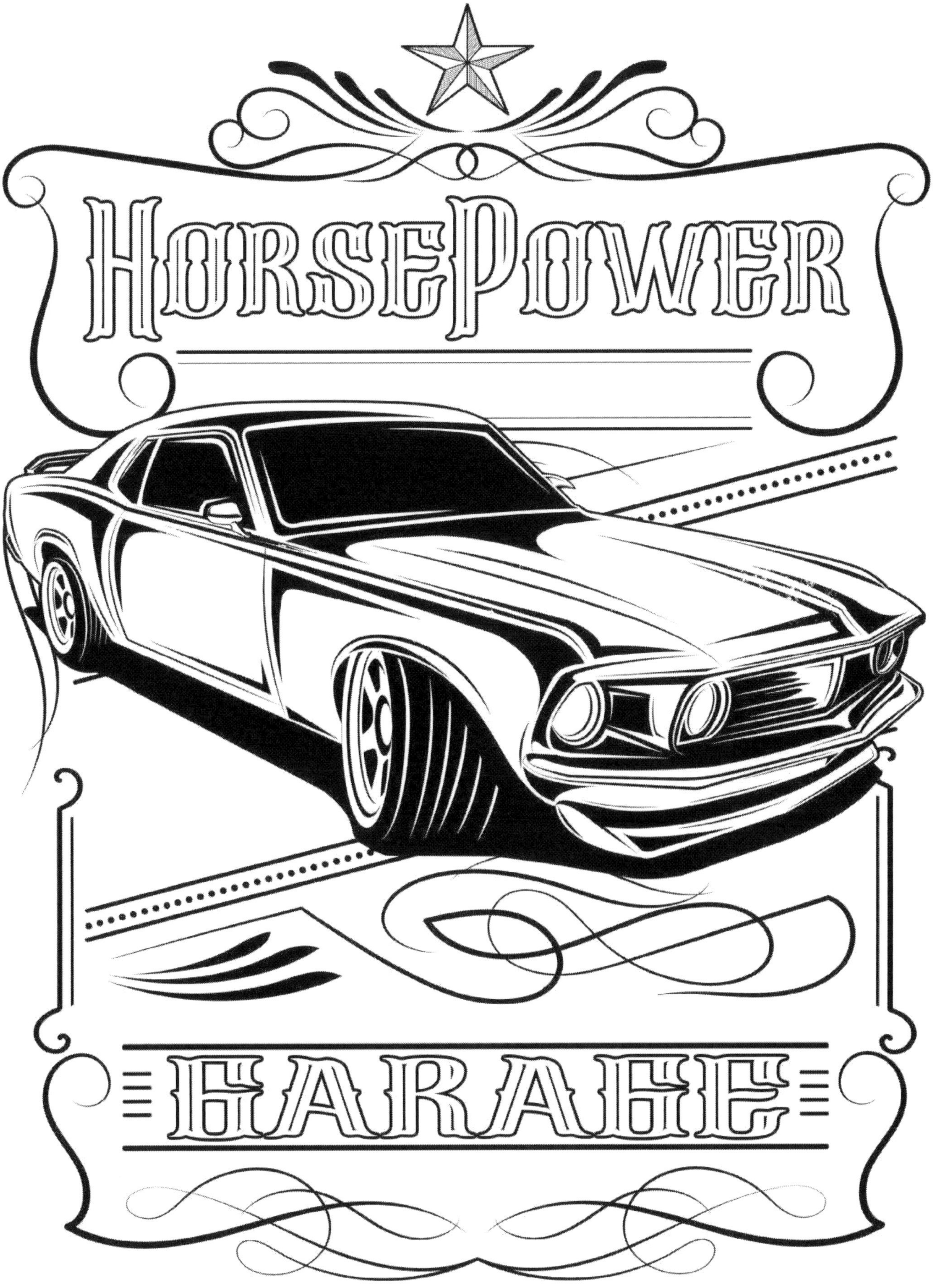
HorsePower
GARAGE

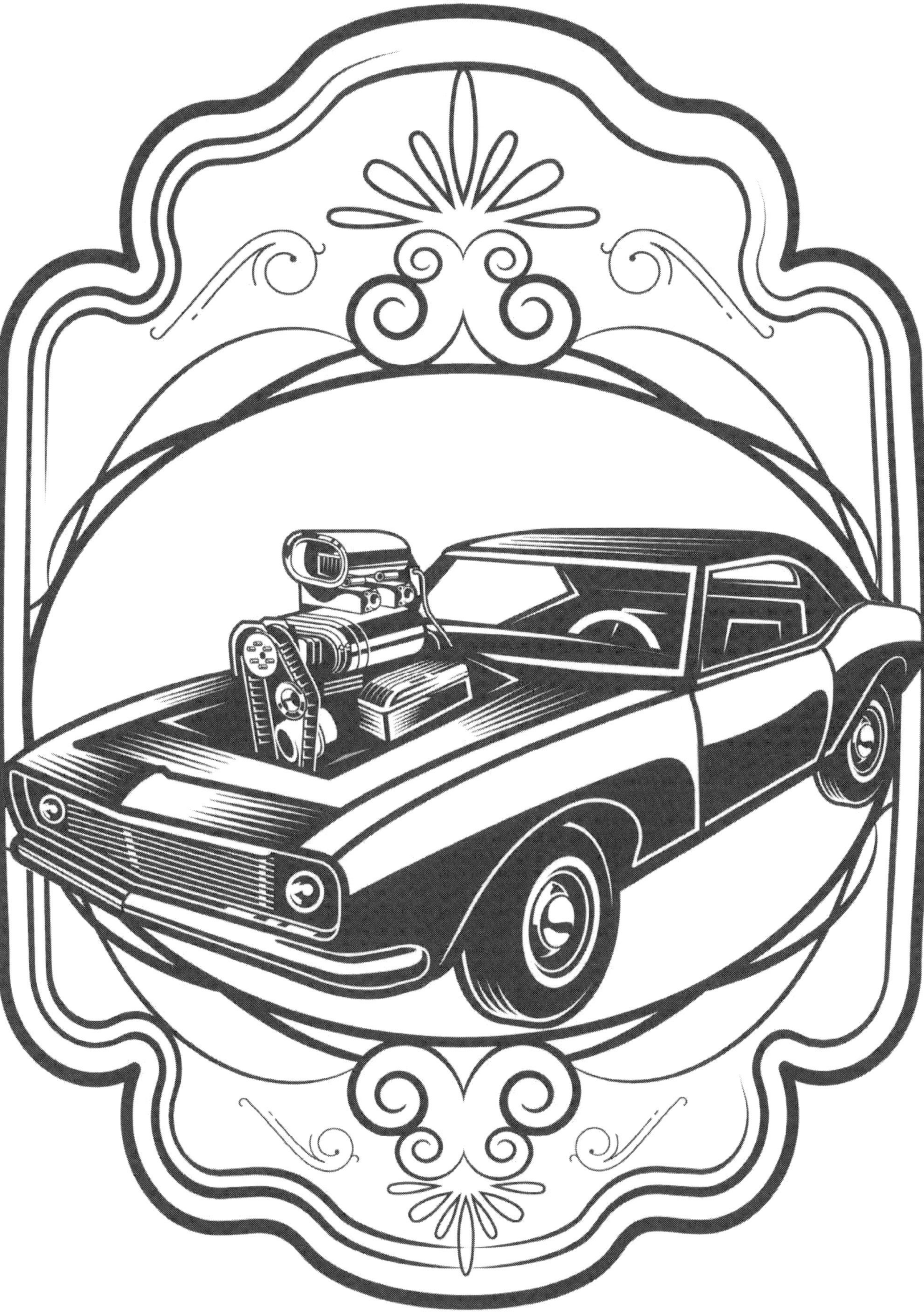

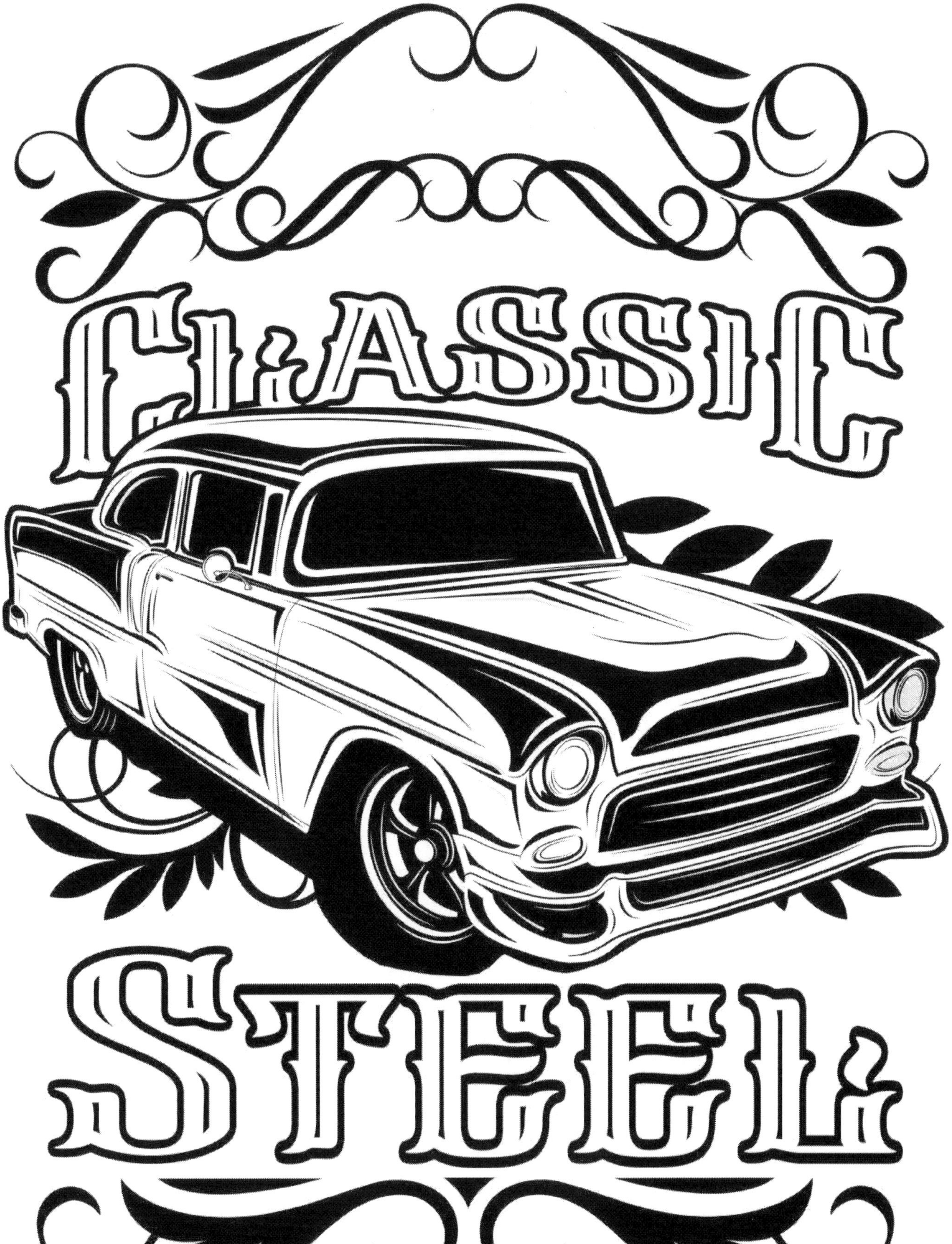
CLASSIC
STEEL

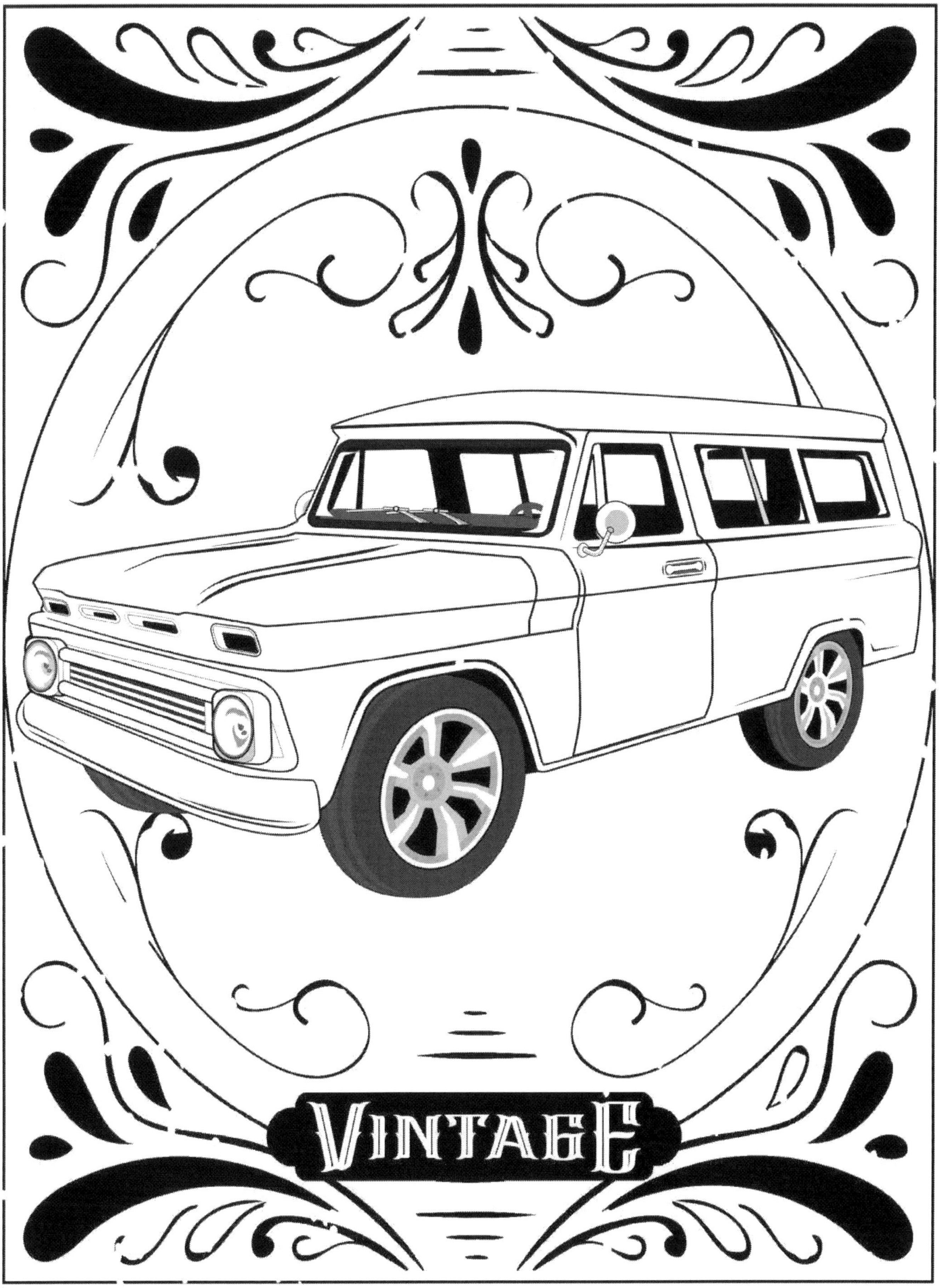
VINTAGE

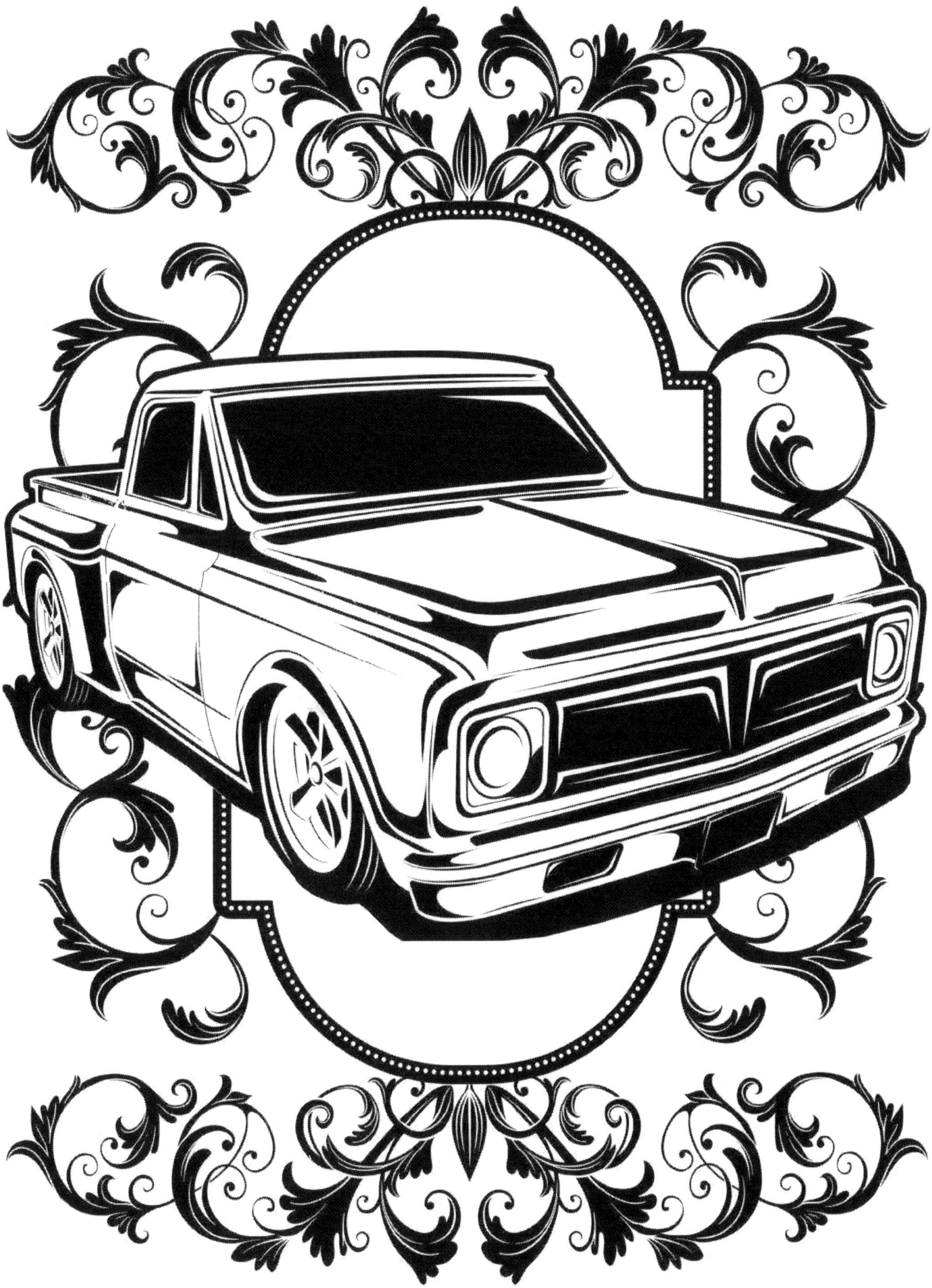

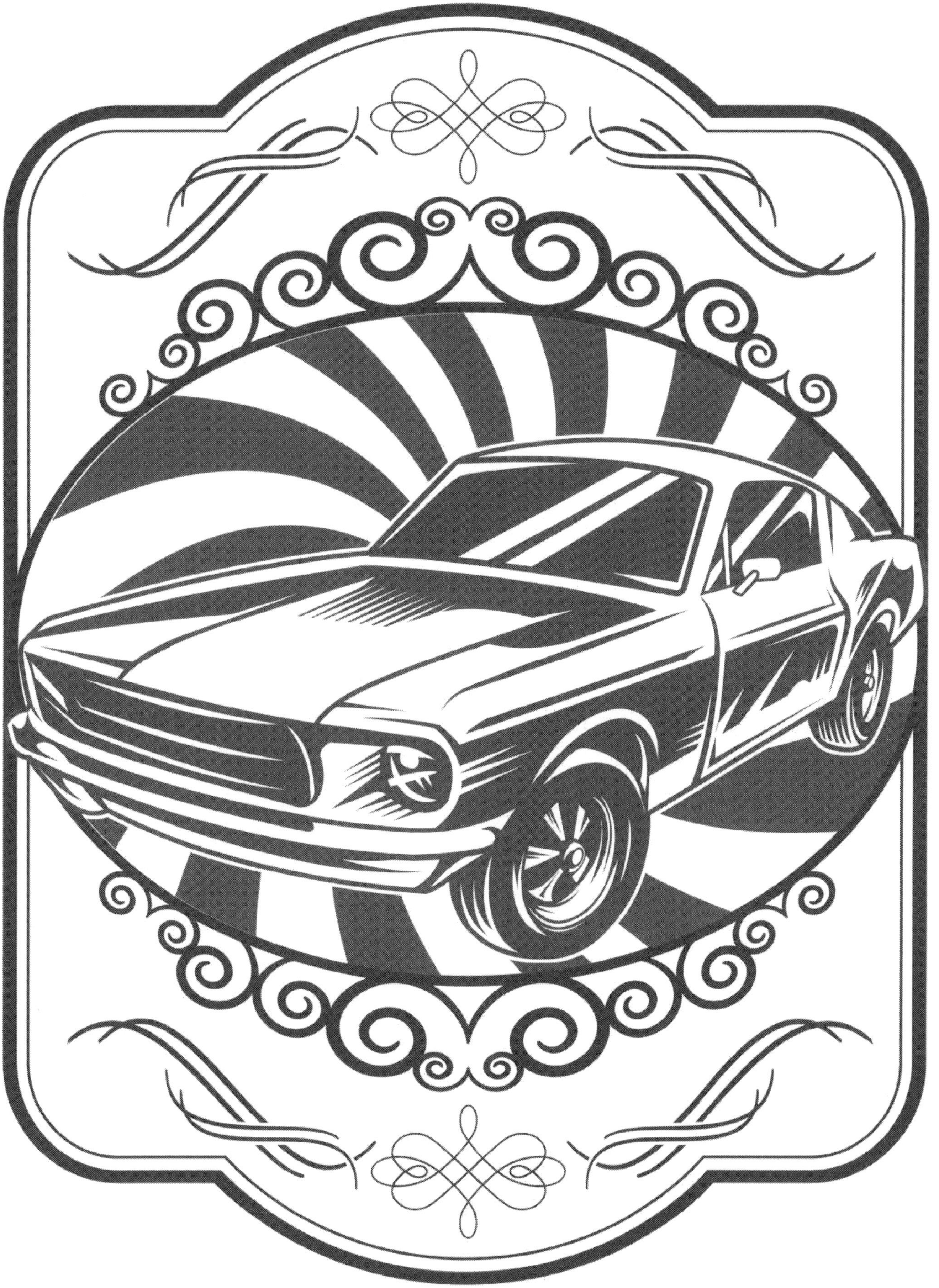

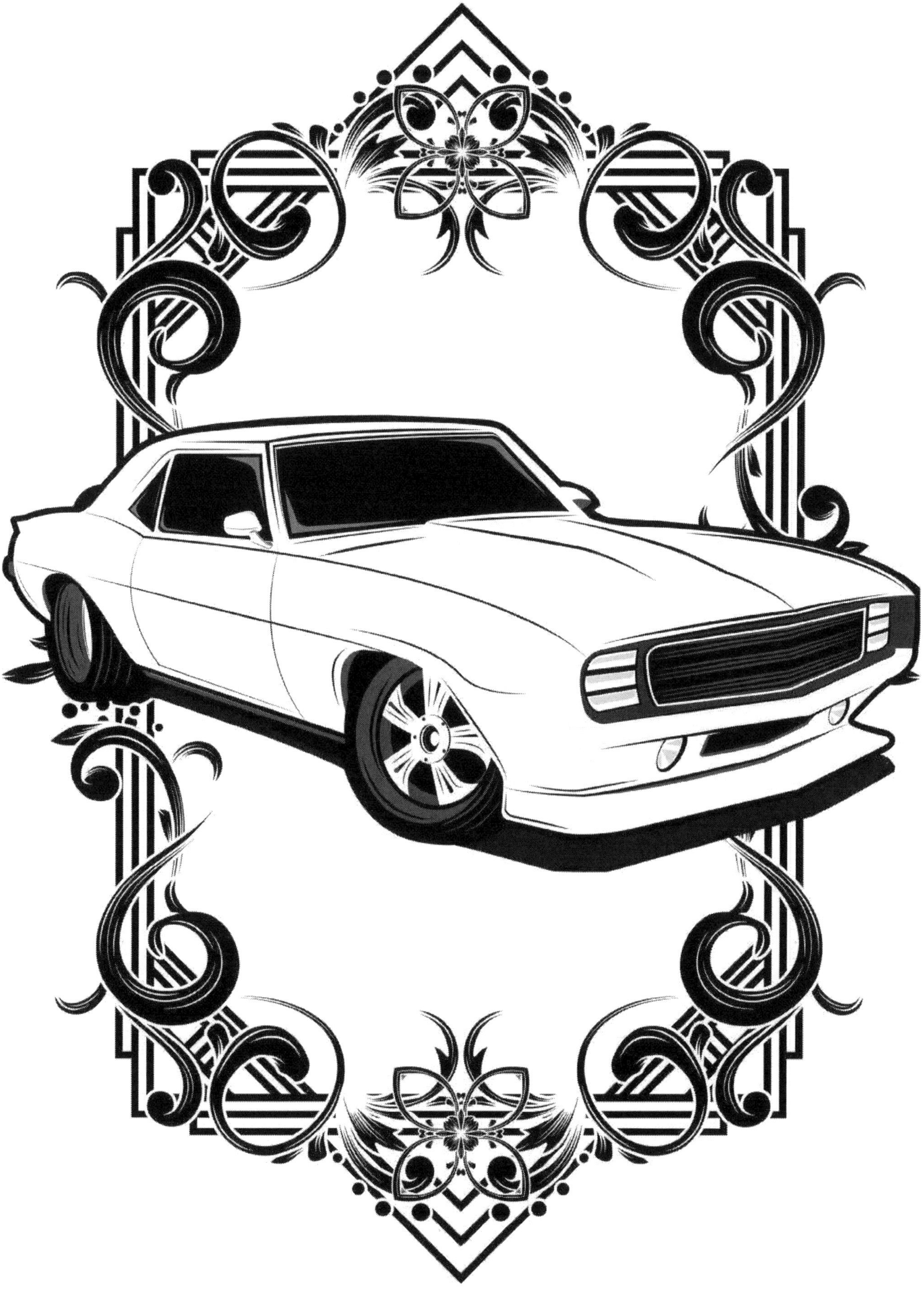

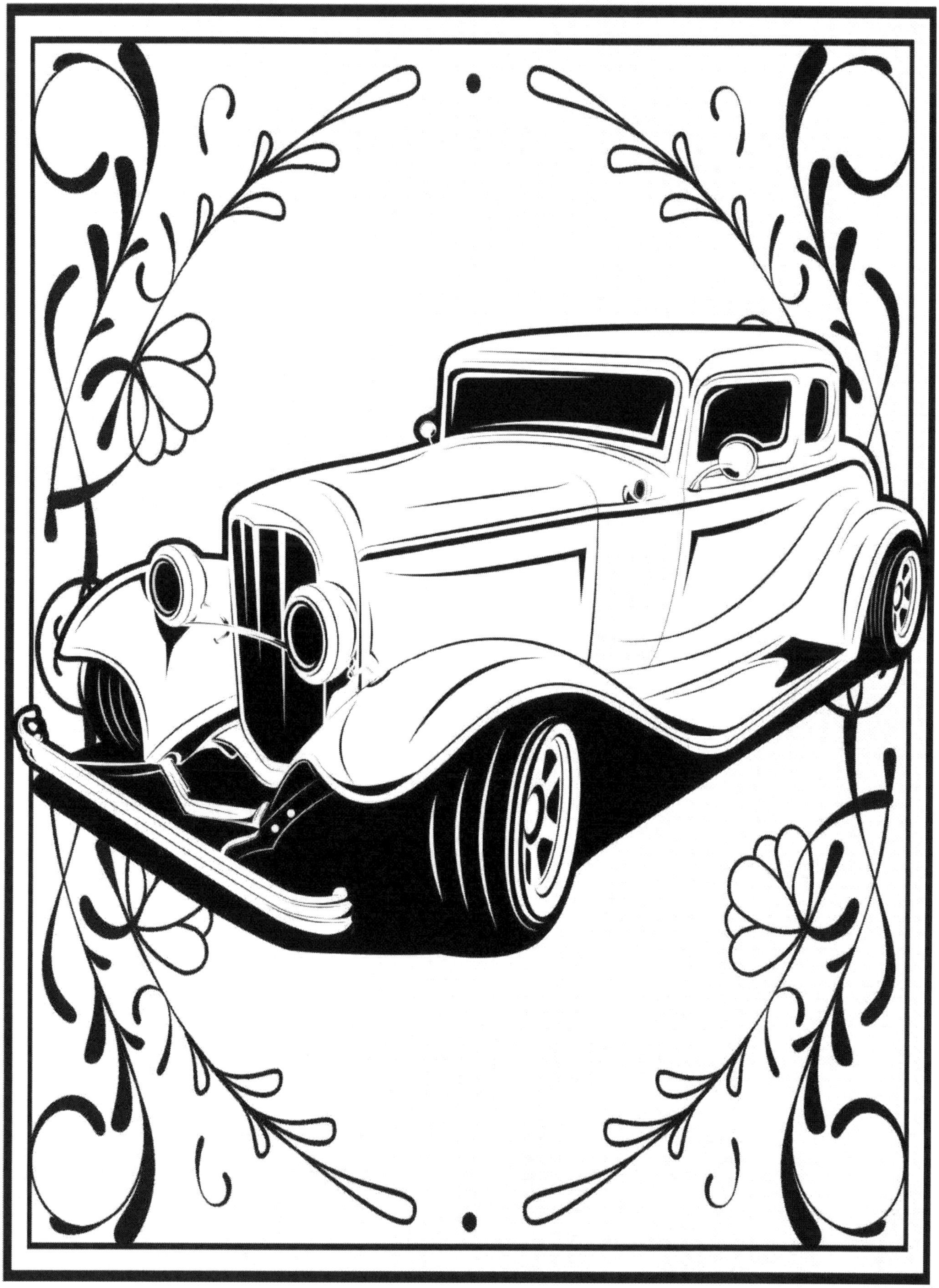

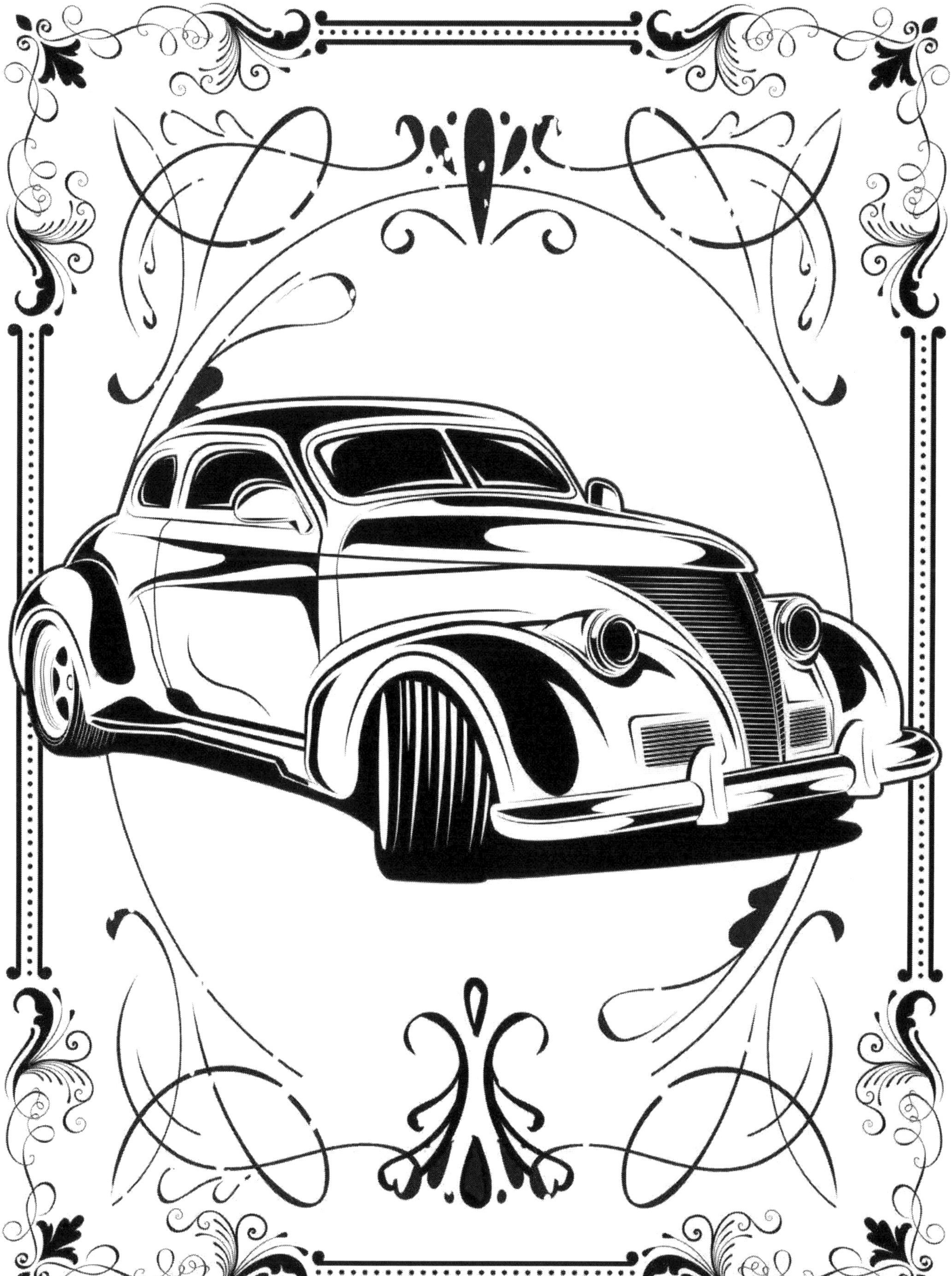

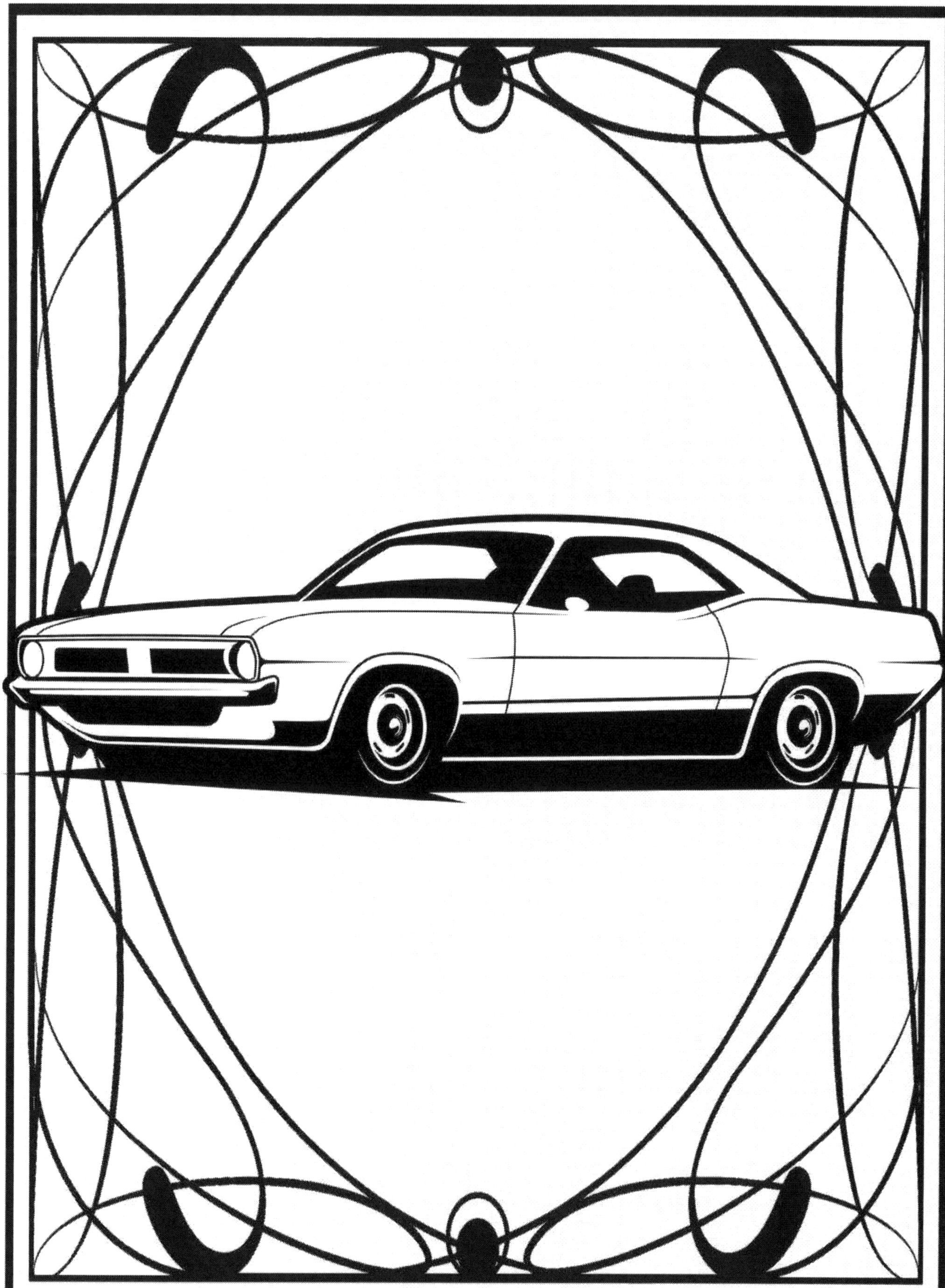

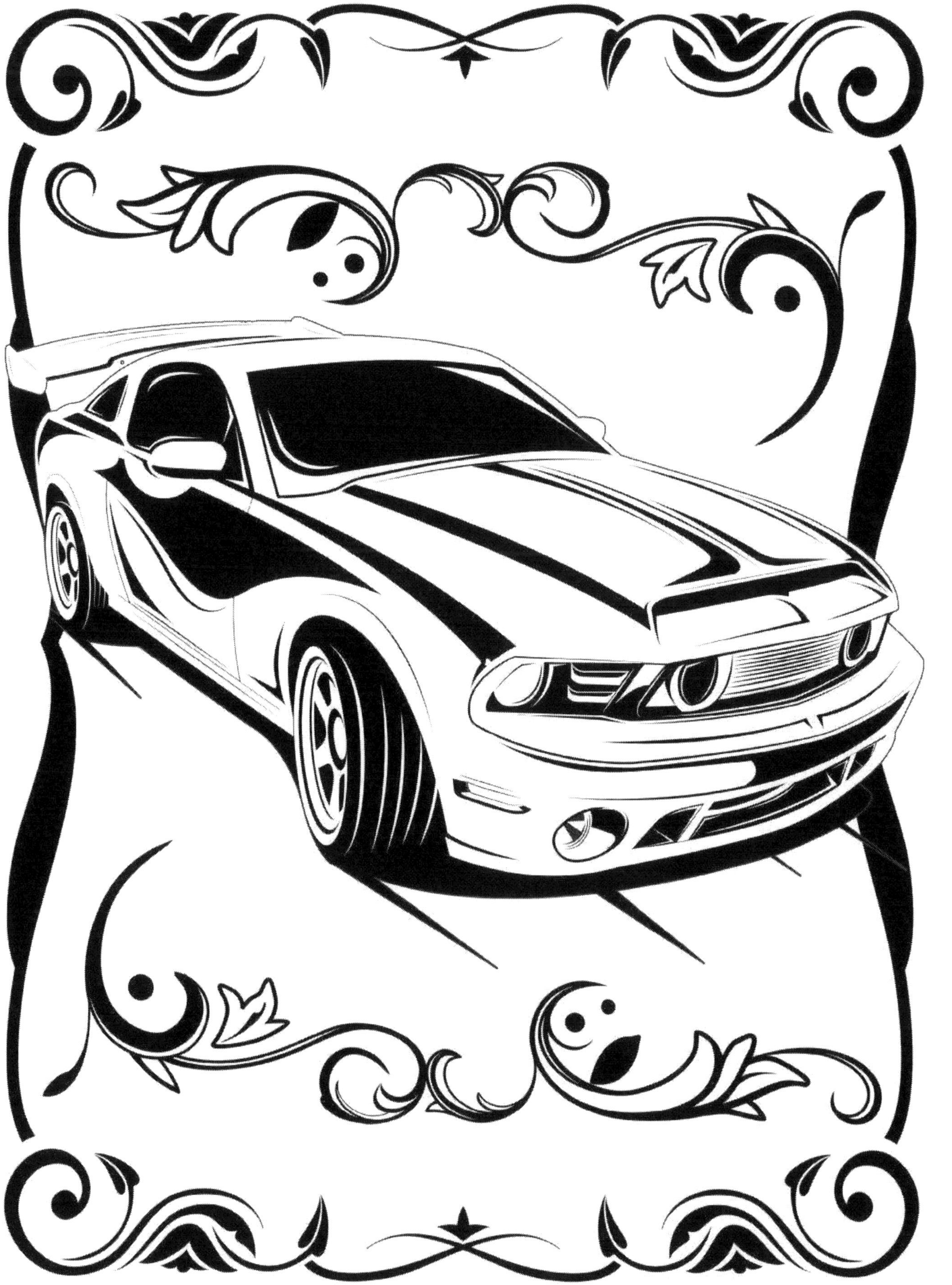

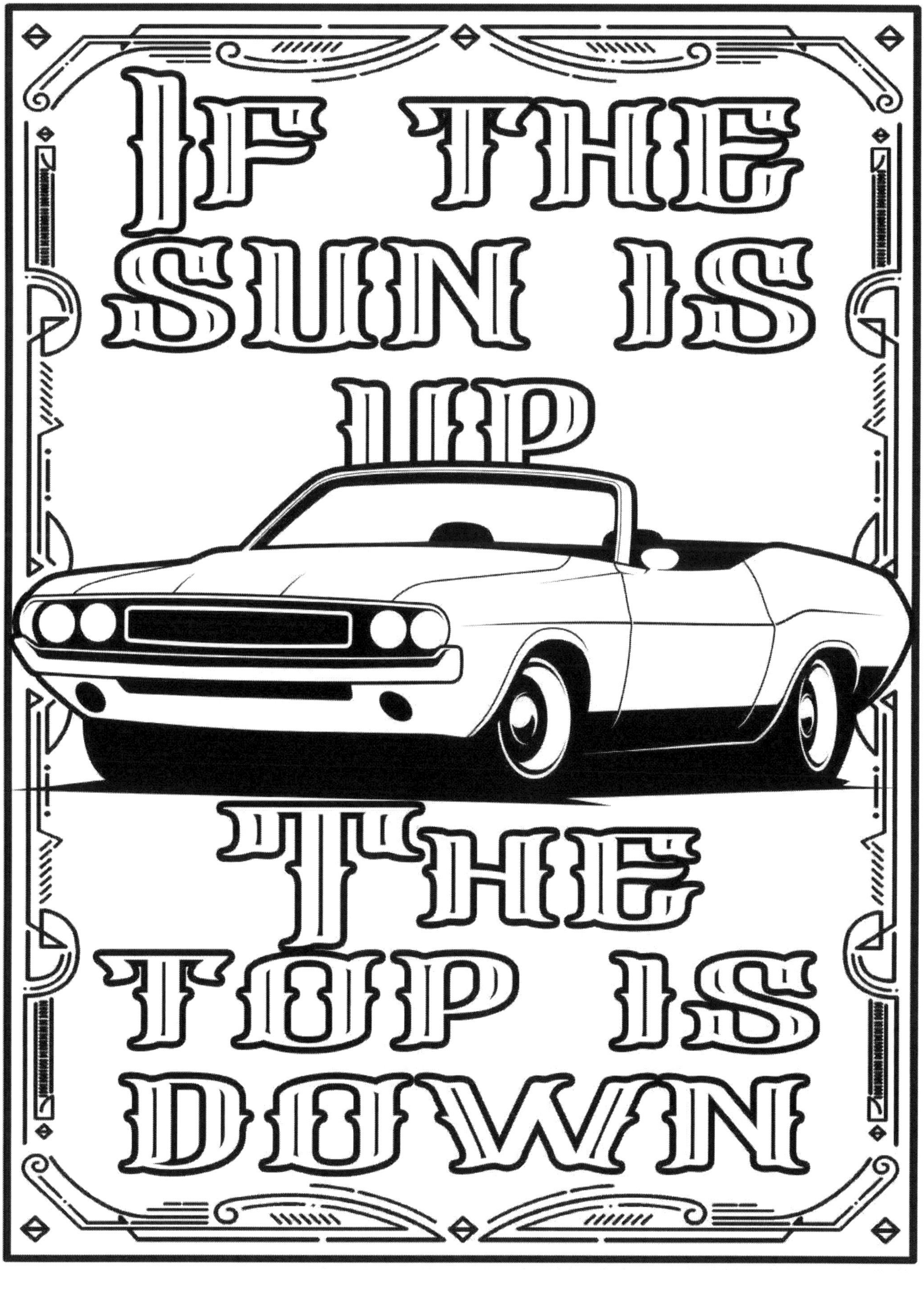
IF THE
SUN IS
UP
THE
TOP IS
DOWN

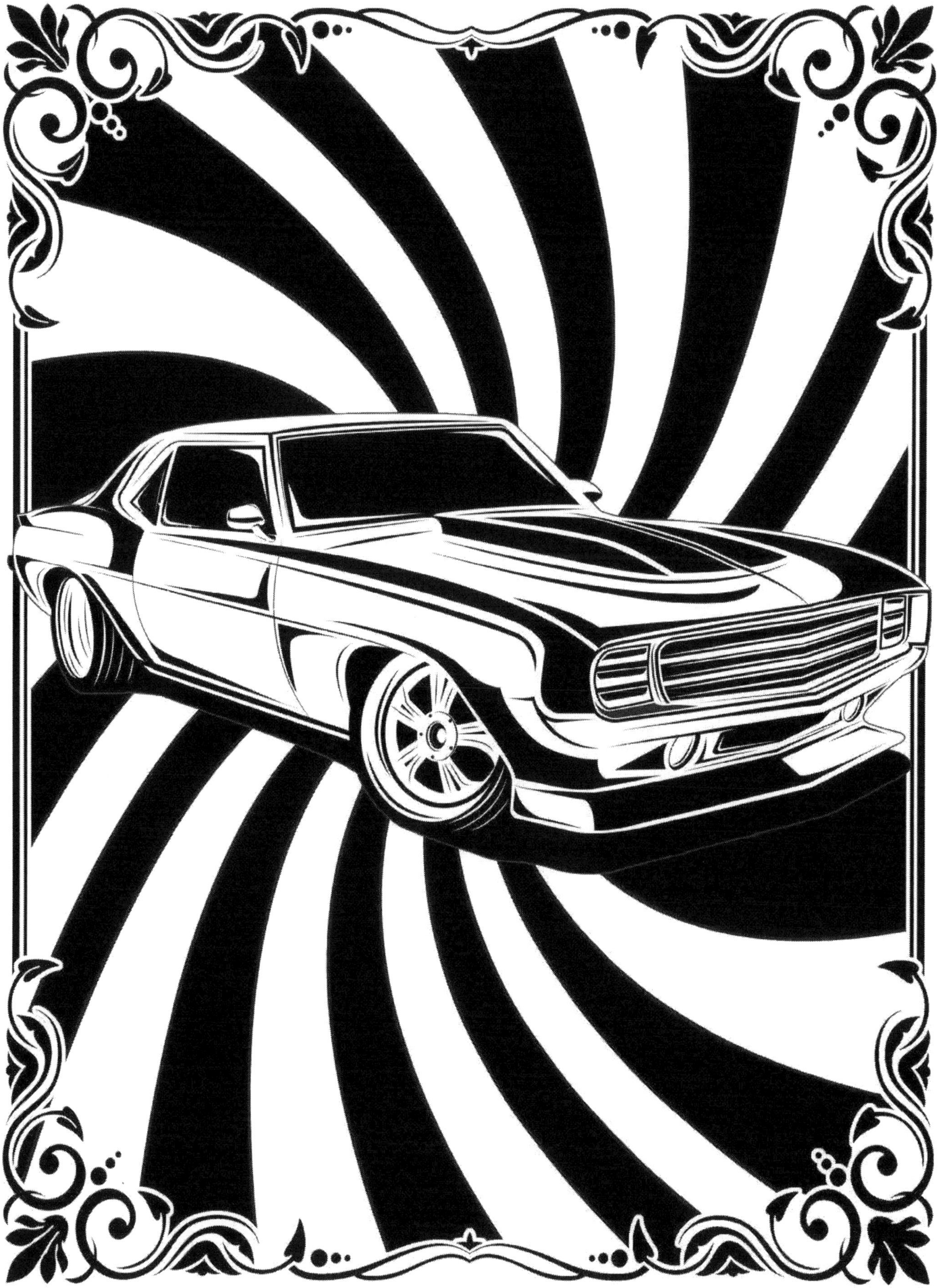

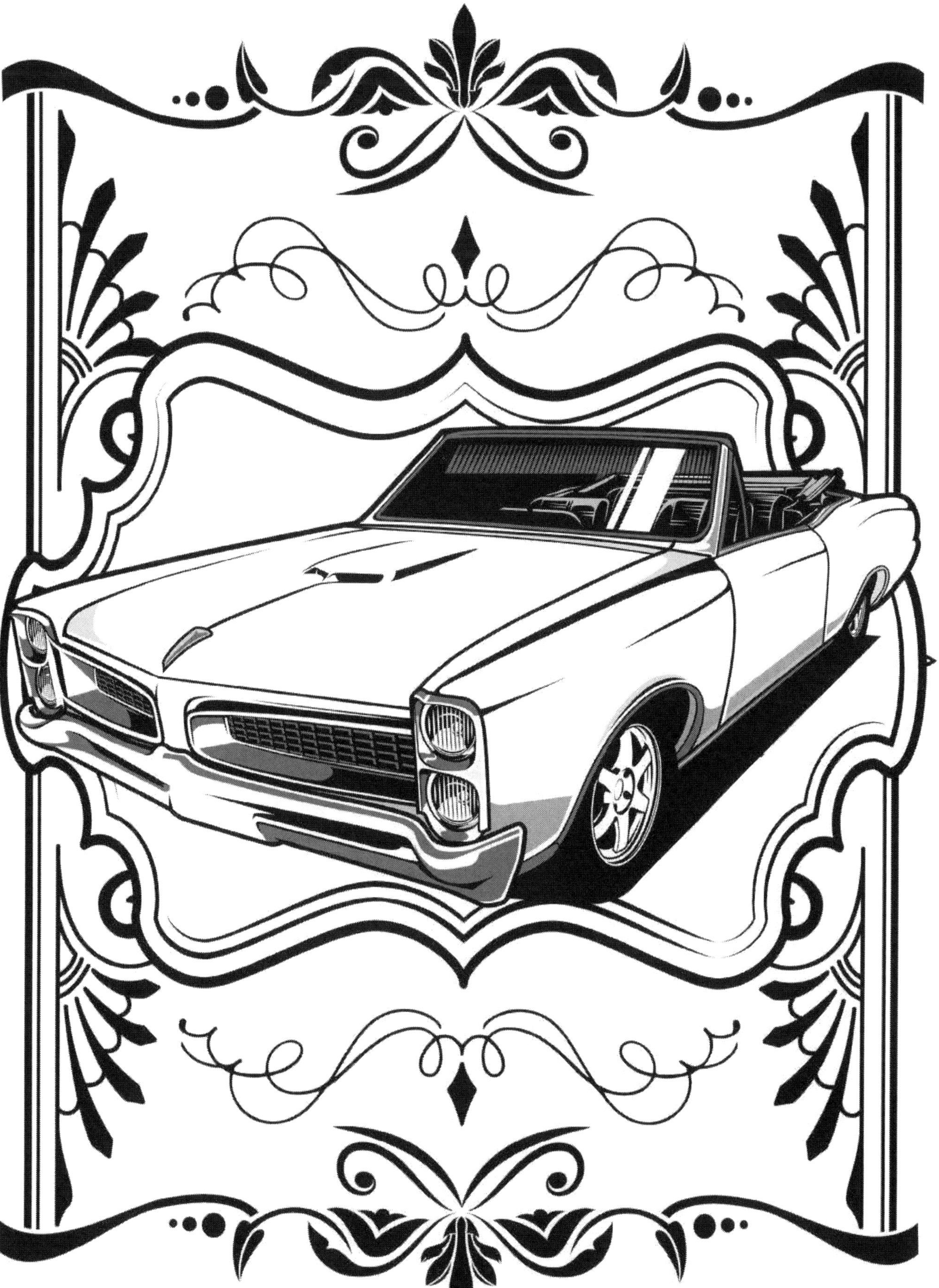

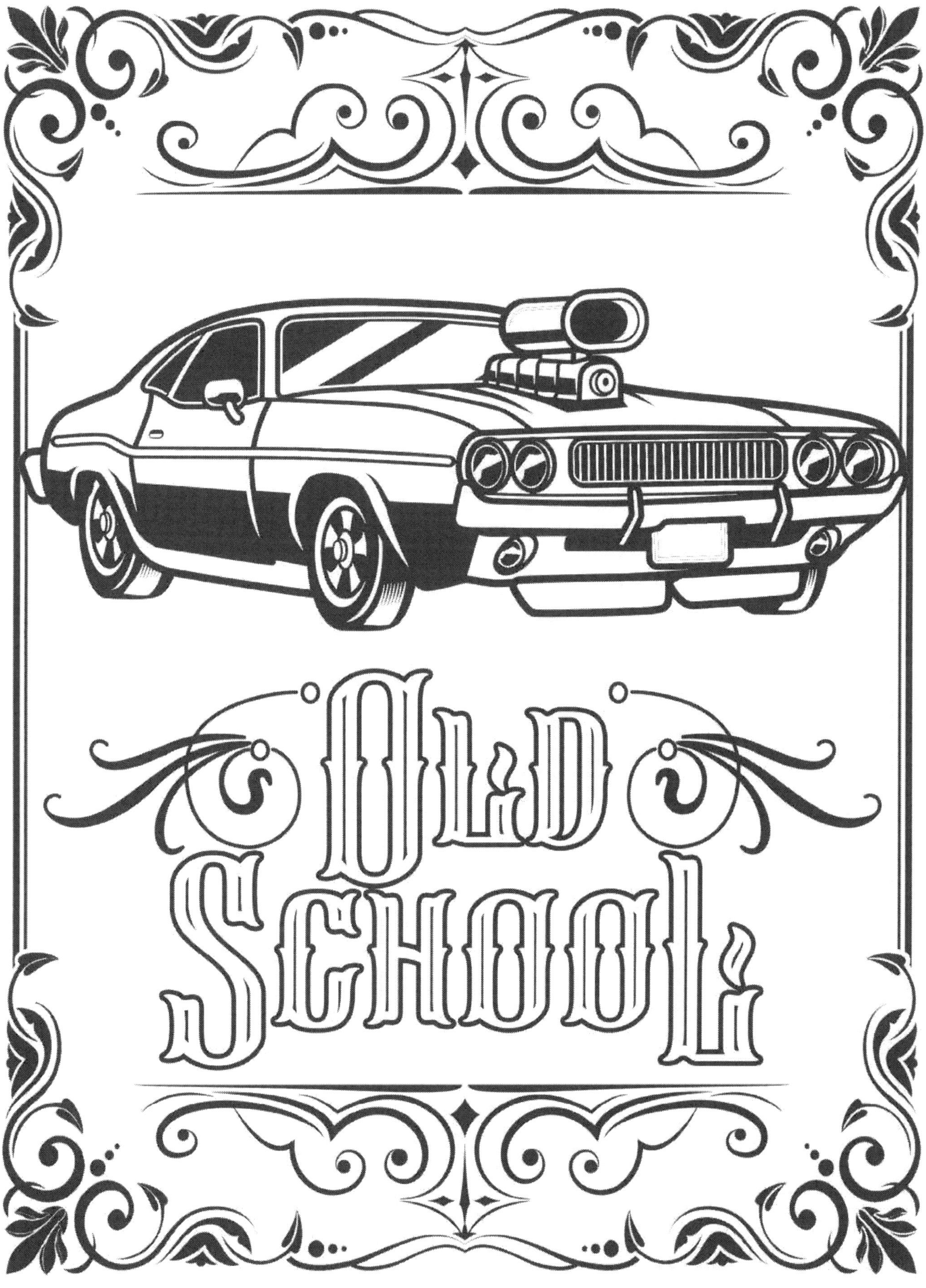
Old
School

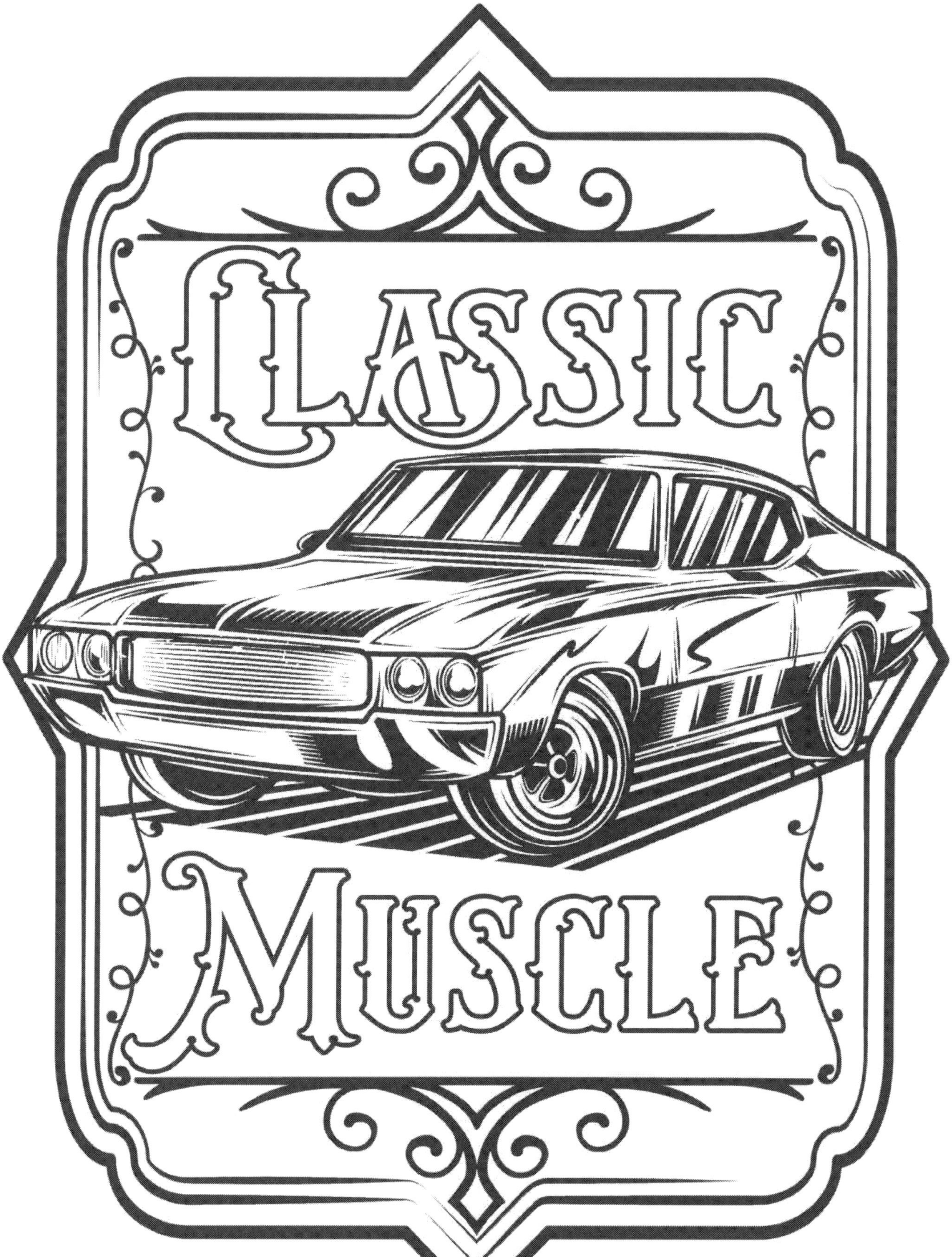
CLASSIC
MUSCLE

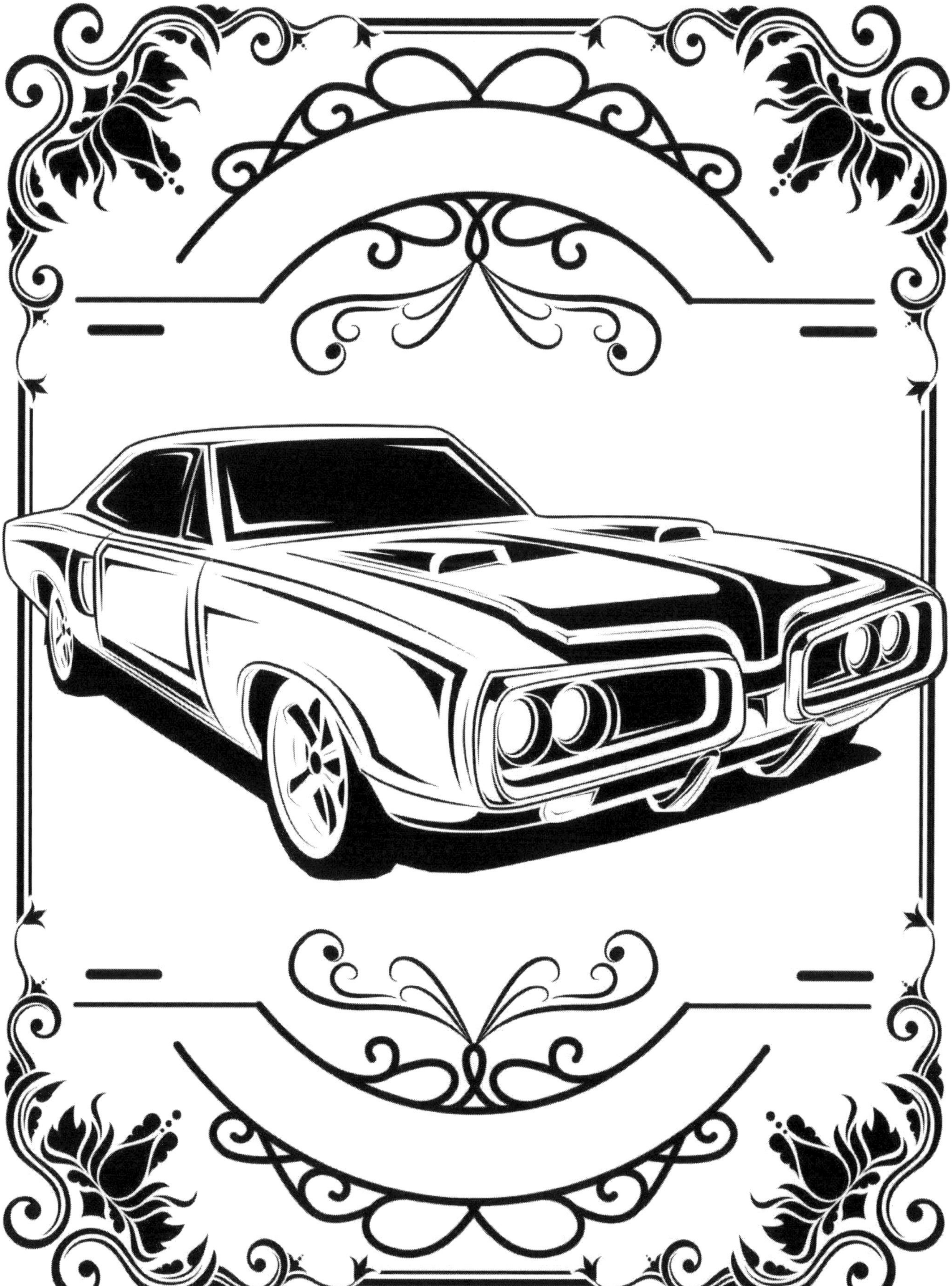

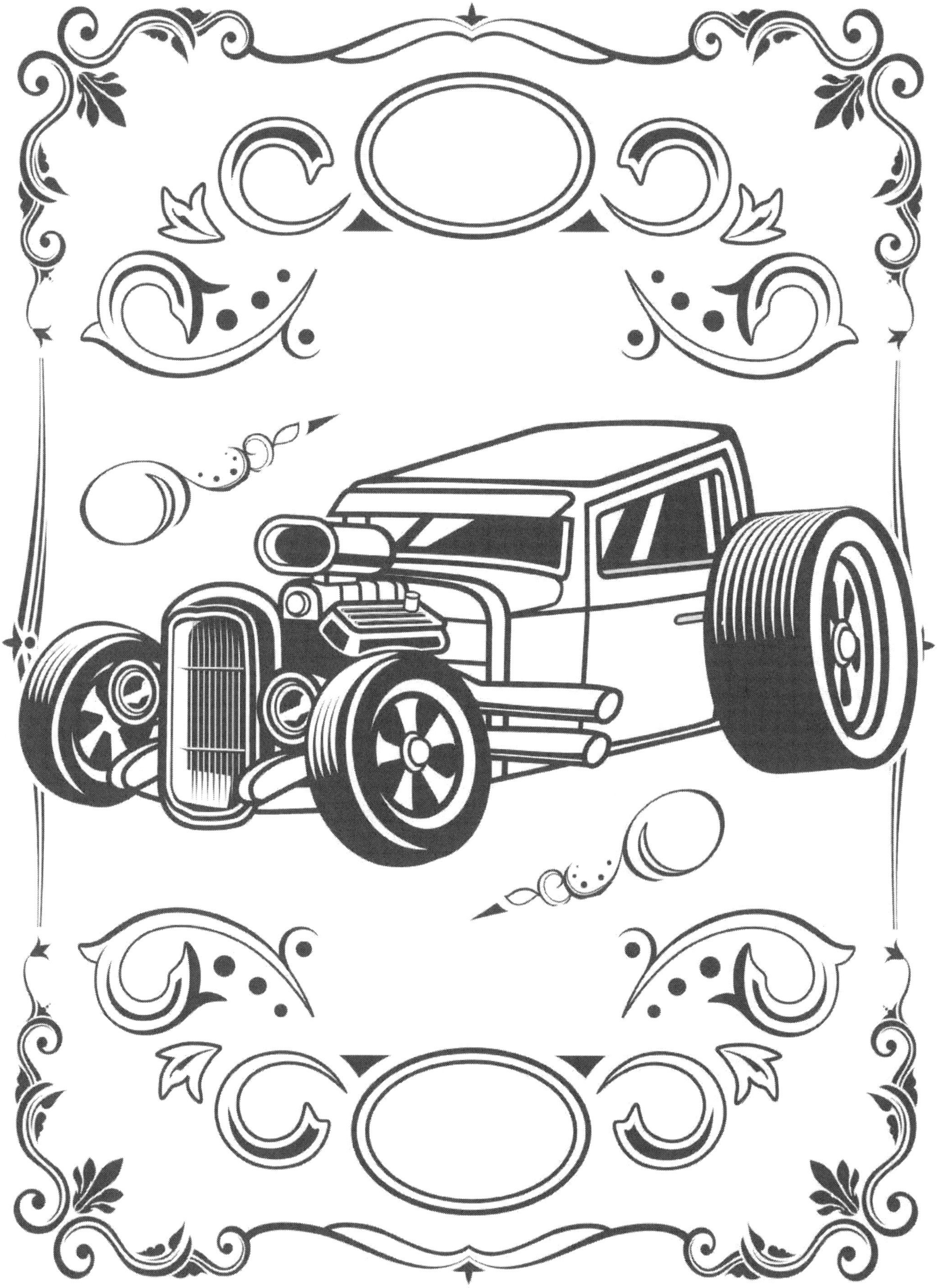

Made in the USA
Las Vegas, NV
02 November 2023

80118520R00032